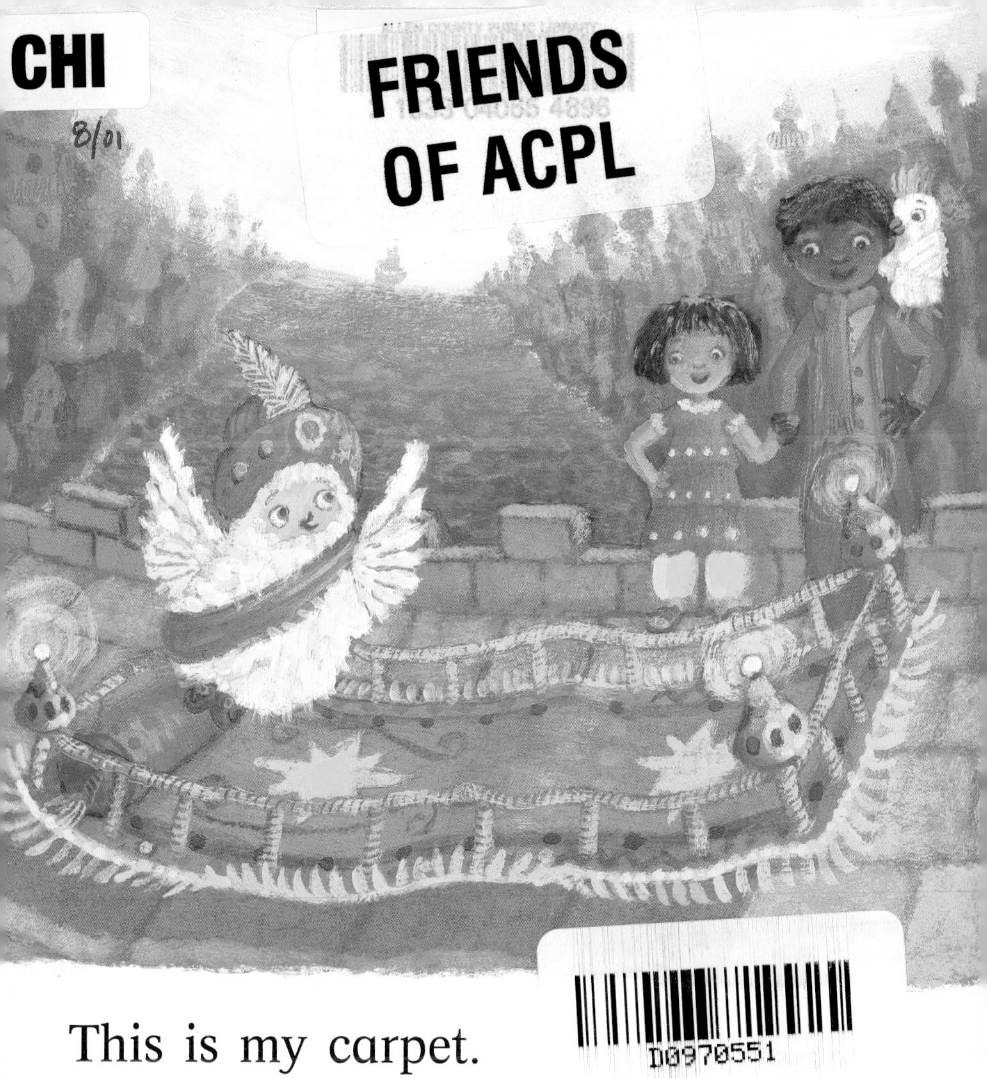

This is my carpet.

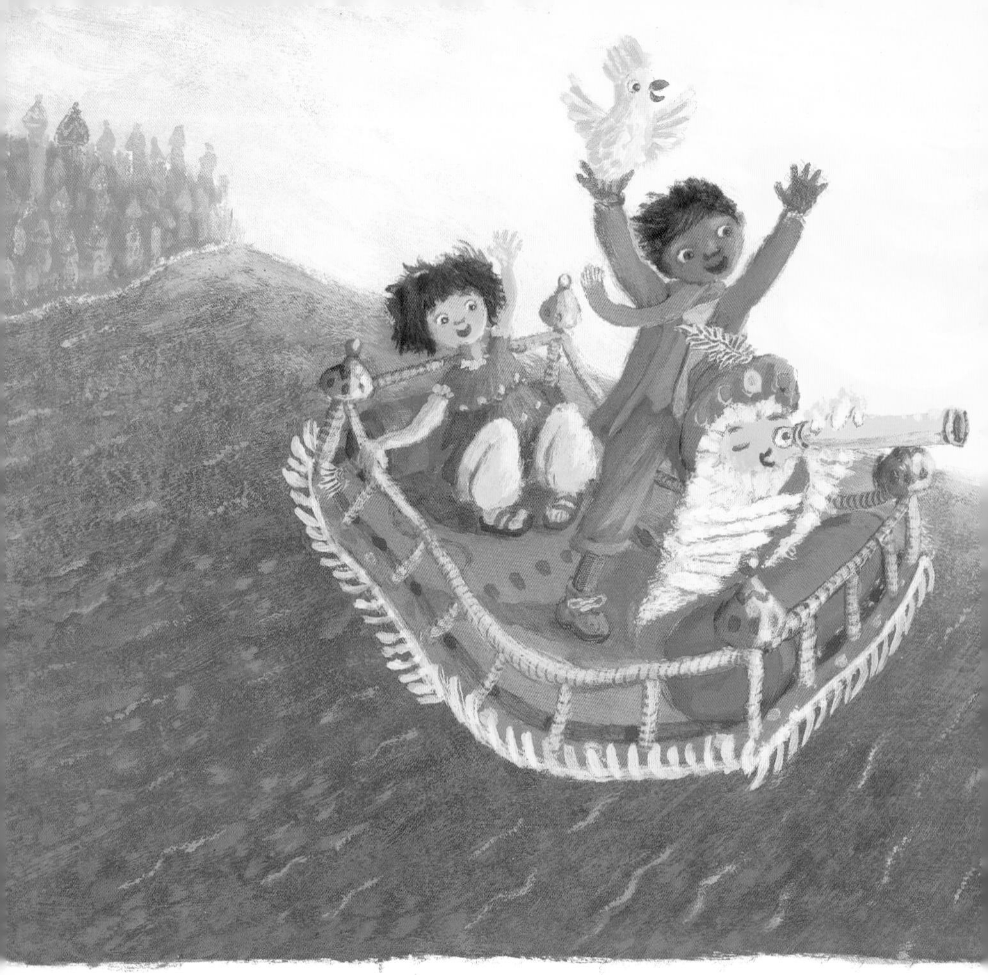

Off we go!

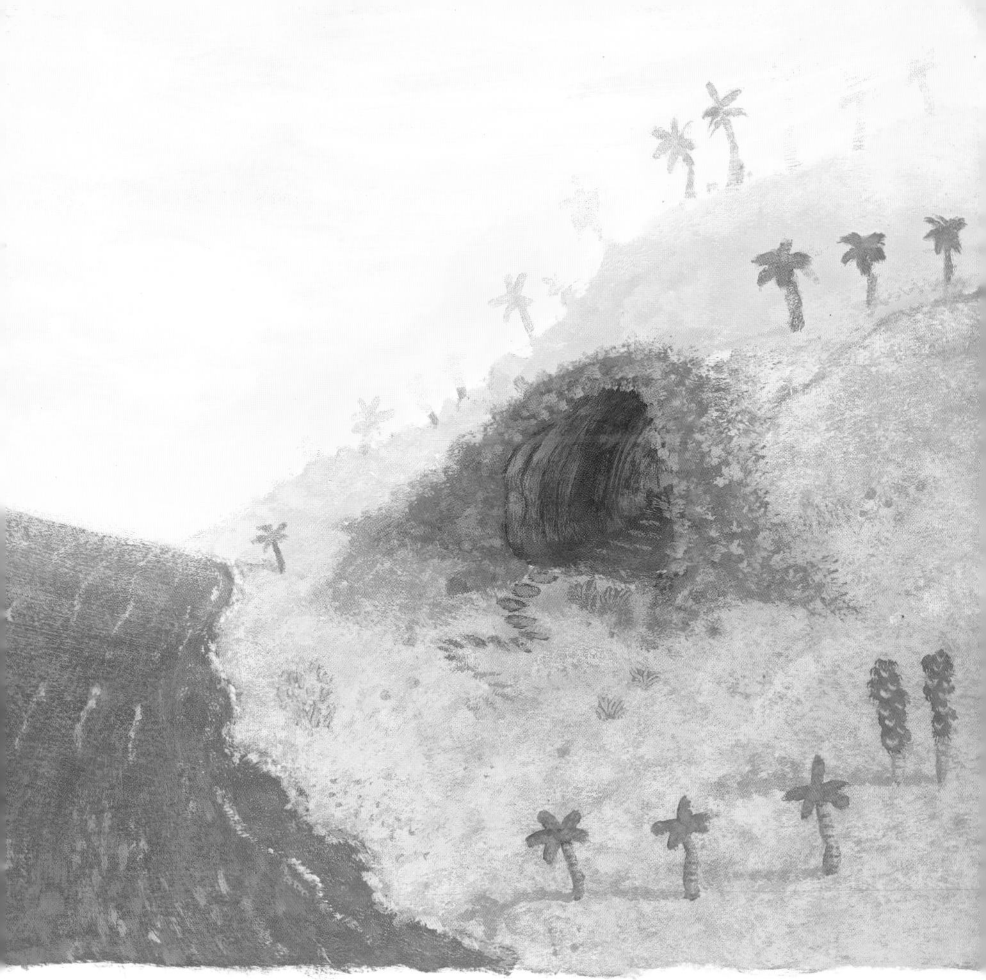

Look at the cave!

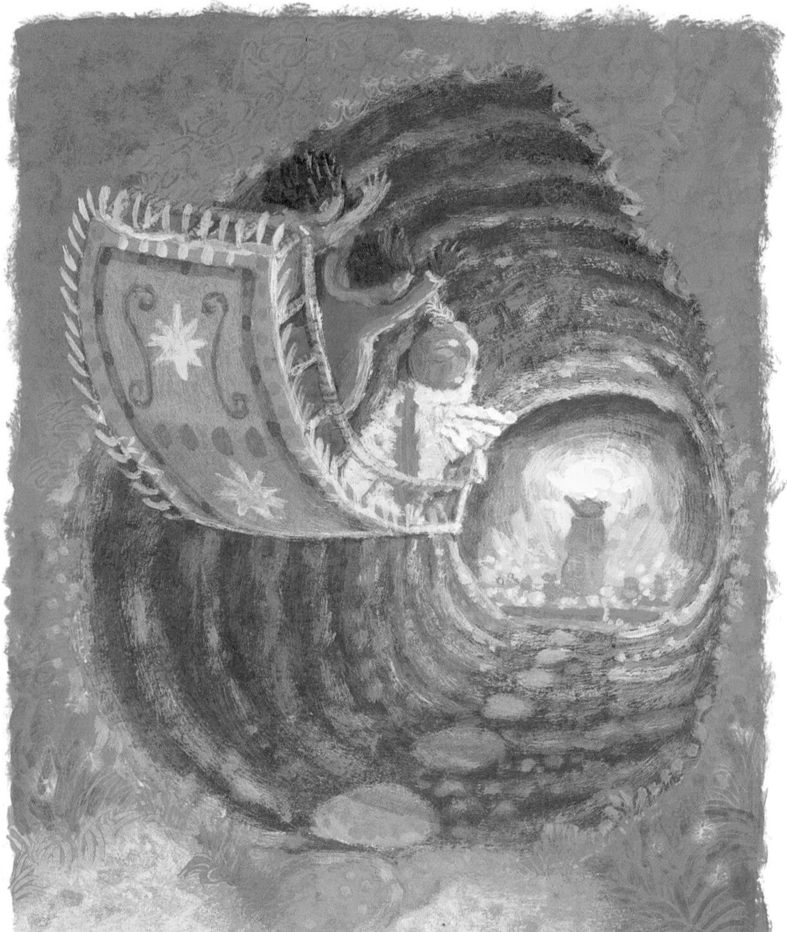

In we go!

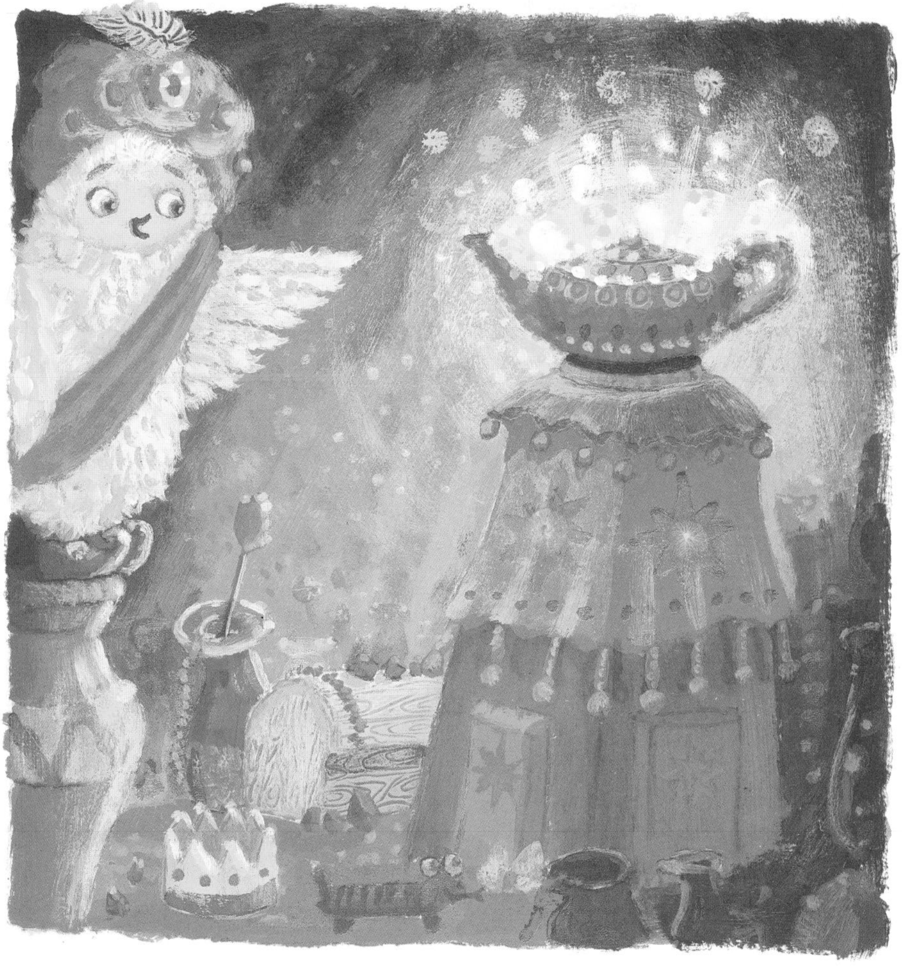

Look! A lamp!

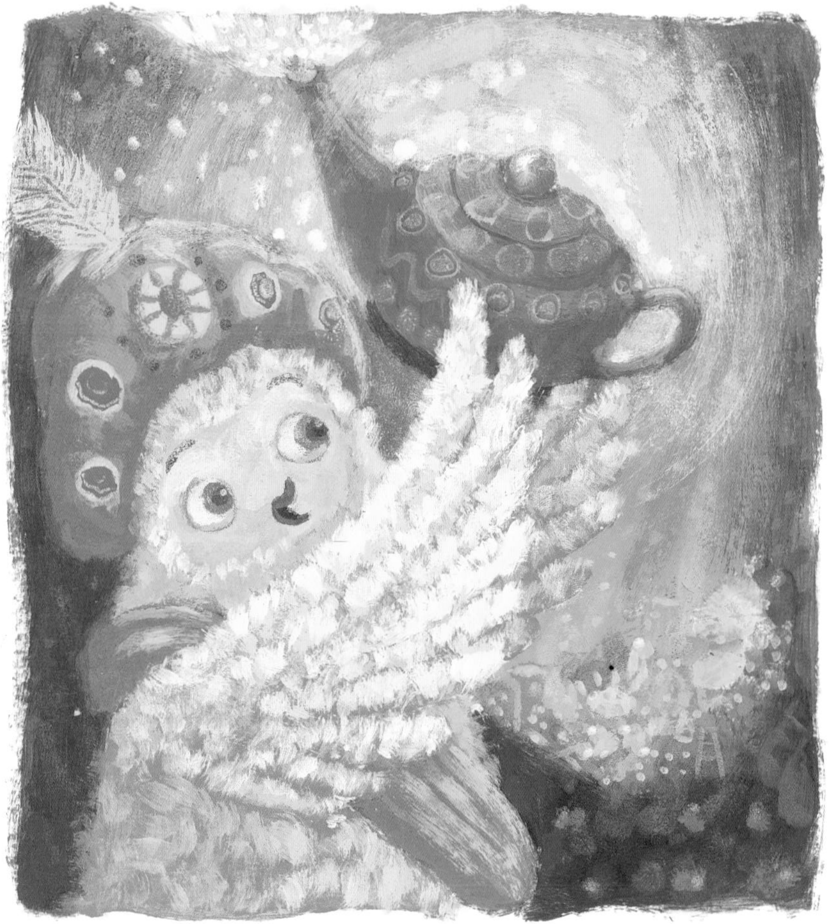

I like this lamp.

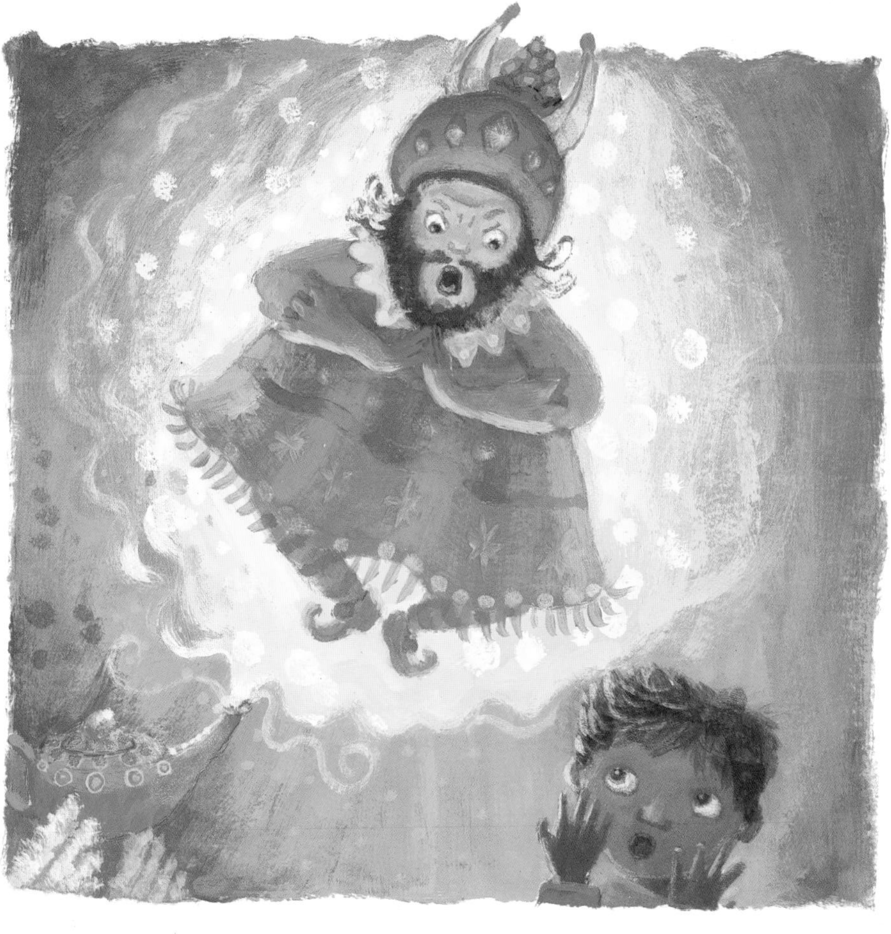

Look at the genie!

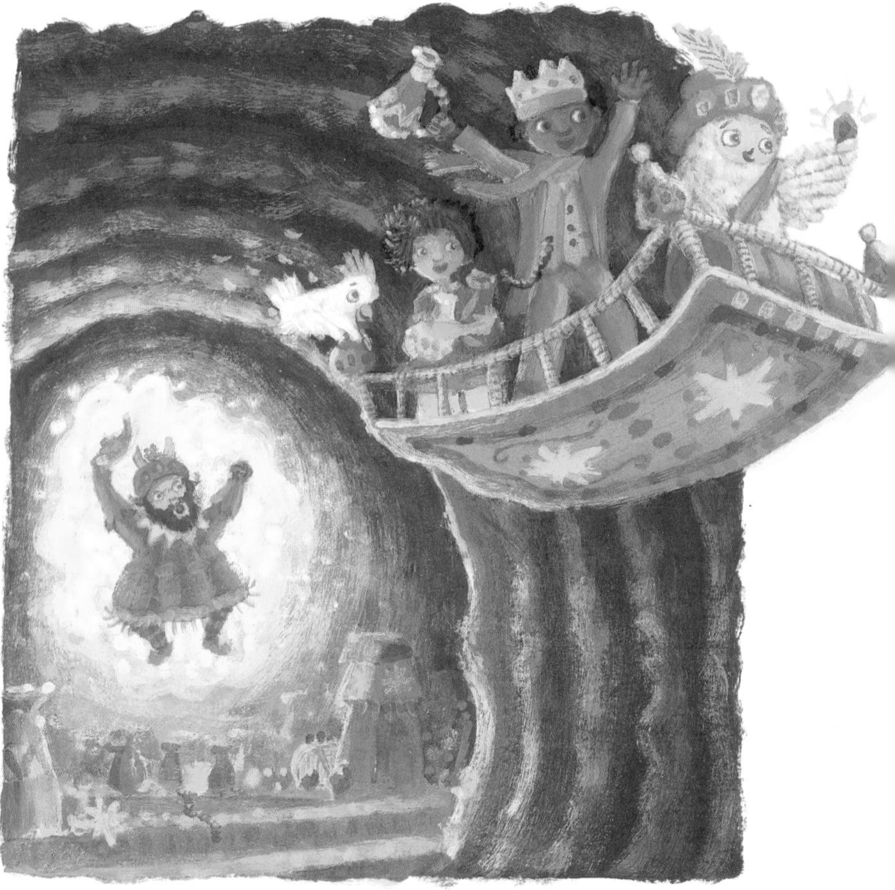

Off we go!